The Fox and the Crow

Retold by Sarah O'Neil
Illustrated by Liz Cogley

sundance
A Haights Cross Communications ◆® Company

A crow found a piece of cheese.

"I'd like to eat that cheese,"
she said.

2

A fox saw the crow
with the piece of cheese.

"I'd like to eat that cheese,"
he said.

The crow flew up into the tree.

The fox sat down under the tree.

"Crow," called the fox.

"May I have some of your cheese?"

The crow kept her beak closed and held on to the cheese.

The fox thought of a plan.

"Crow," he called.
"I see that you have
beautiful black wing feathers —
the finest wings in the land."

The crow listened and was happy.

But she kept her beak closed
and held on to the cheese.

"Crow," he called.
"I see that you have
beautiful black tail feathers —
the finest tail in the land."

The crow listened
and was very happy.

But she kept her beak closed
and held on to the cheese.

"Crow," he called.

"I hear that you have
a beautiful singing voice —
the finest voice in the land.
Is this true?" asked the fox.

15

The crow listened
and was so happy
that she opened her beak
and began to sing.

The cheese fell to the ground,
and the fox gobbled it up.